PRINCEWILL LAGANG

The Legacy of L'Oreal: Francoise Bettencourt Meyers and the Business of Beauty

First published by PRINCEWILL LAGANG 2023

Copyright © 2023 by Princewill Lagang

All rights reserved. No part of this publication may be reproduced, stored or transmitted in any form or by any means, electronic, mechanical, photocopying, recording, scanning, or otherwise without written permission from the publisher. It is illegal to copy this book, post it to a website, or distribute it by any other means without permission.

Princewill Lagang asserts the moral right to be identified as the author of this work.

First edition

This book was professionally typeset on Reedsy.
Find out more at reedsy.com

Contents

1 Introduction — 1
2 The Legacy of L'Oreal: Francoise Bettencourt Meyers and the — 3
3 Roots of Innovation: L'Oreal's Evolution in the Beauty... — 6
4 Navigating Beauty's New Horizon: Francoise Bettencourt... — 8
5 Sculpting Beauty with Purpose: L'Oreal's Social... — 10
6 Innovation Beyond Borders: L'Oreal's Global Impact and the... — 12
7 The Tapestry Unfurls: L'Oreal's Cultural Impact and Shaping... — 14
8 The Future Canvas: Francoise Bettencourt Meyers' Vision for... — 16
9 Legacy in Bloom: Reflections, Continuity, and the... — 18
10 Eternal Beauty: L'Oreal's Timeless Impact and the... — 20
11 A Timeless Elegance: The Unfolding Legacy and Future... — 22
12 Legacy Unbound: L'Oreal's Ongoing Journey and the... — 24
13 Eternal Beauty: The Legacy Lives On — 27
14 Summary — 29

1

Introduction

Welcome to "The Legacy of L'Oreal: Francoise Bettencourt Meyers and the Business of Beauty," a captivating exploration into the heart and soul of one of the world's most iconic beauty brands. In the following pages, we embark on a journey through time, tracing the footsteps of L'Oreal from its modest beginnings to its current status as a global beauty powerhouse.

This narrative unfolds as a tapestry, interweaving history, innovation, and the visionary leadership of Francoise Bettencourt Meyers, who has not only steered the company through changing tides but has also redefined beauty narratives for a new era.

Join us as we delve into the early days of L'Oreal, discovering the innovative spirit that birthed some of the industry's most iconic products. Follow the company's evolution through global expansion, exploring the cultural impact that has made L'Oreal a symbol of empowerment and self-expression.

Throughout this journey, we will shine a spotlight on Francoise Bettencourt Meyers, the stalwart leader at the helm of L'Oreal. Uncover her unique approach to leadership, her commitment to sustainability and social responsibility, and her vision for the future of beauty.

THE LEGACY OF L'OREAL: FRANCOISE BETTENCOURT MEYERS AND THE BUSINESS OF BEAUTY

"The Legacy of L'Oreal" is not just a story about cosmetics; it is a narrative that transcends time, touching on themes of culture, innovation, and the transformative power of beauty. So, buckle up as we navigate the chapters of this remarkable legacy, celebrating the enduring influence of L'Oreal on the global stage.

2

The Legacy of L'Oreal: Francoise Bettencourt Meyers and the Business of Beauty

The morning sun bathed the elegant streets of Paris in a warm glow as Francoise Bettencourt Meyers strolled through the historic city. With each step, she carried not only the weight of her family name but also the responsibility of upholding a legacy that stretched across generations. The legacy of L'Oreal.

As the only child of Liliane Bettencourt, the heiress of the L'Oreal empire, Francoise found herself at the intersection of privilege and duty. The world of beauty and cosmetics had been her family's domain for decades, dating back to the inception of L'Oreal in 1909 by her grandfather, Eugene Schueller. The company's rise from a small hair dye manufacturer to a global beauty powerhouse mirrored the transformation of Paris itself.

In this opening chapter, we delve into the rich history of L'Oreal, exploring its humble beginnings and the visionary leadership that propelled it to international acclaim. Eugene Schueller's passion for innovation laid the foundation for a company that would revolutionize the beauty industry. His early experiments with hair dyes and commitment to quality set the stage for L'Oreal's future success.

The narrative then shifts to the post-war era when Liliane Bettencourt took the reins of the company. Her unwavering dedication and business acumen expanded L'Oreal's reach beyond French borders, turning it into a global icon. The acquisition of iconic brands, the development of groundbreaking products, and a commitment to research and development marked Liliane's tenure at the helm.

As we explore L'Oreal's trajectory, we also unravel the complexities of being a business magnate in the world of beauty. The challenges faced, the industry dynamics, and the relentless pursuit of perfection in an ever-evolving market become integral parts of the story.

The narrative takes an intimate turn as we delve into the life of Francoise Bettencourt Meyers. Raised amidst the opulence of the Bettencourt estate, she developed a profound appreciation for the artistry and science that defined L'Oreal. However, her journey wasn't without its share of trials. We explore her early years, her education, and the pivotal moments that shaped her worldview.

The chapter concludes with a present-day glimpse into Francoise's role as the chairwoman of L'Oreal and her commitment to sustainability, innovation, and social responsibility. The stage is set for a compelling exploration of how Francoise Bettencourt Meyers navigates the delicate balance between tradition and progress, heritage and innovation, in steering the ship of L'Oreal into the future.

Through meticulous research, insightful interviews, and a narrative that seamlessly weaves together history, biography, and business analysis, Chapter 1 sets the tone for a captivating journey into "The Legacy of L'Oreal: Francoise

Bettencourt Meyers and the Business of Beauty."

3

Roots of Innovation: L'Oreal's Evolution in the Beauty Landscape

In the hallowed halls of L'Oreal's research and development laboratories, a symphony of creativity and scientific inquiry played out. Chapter 2 of "The Legacy of L'Oreal: Francoise Bettencourt Meyers and the Business of Beauty" delves deep into the roots of innovation that have defined L'Oreal's ascent to the summit of the beauty industry.

The chapter opens with a vivid exploration of L'Oreal's commitment to research and development. From the groundbreaking inventions of Eugene Schueller to the cutting-edge laboratories of the present day, the company's ethos of pushing the boundaries of beauty is showcased. We uncover the secrets behind iconic product launches, scientific breakthroughs, and the tireless pursuit of excellence that has made L'Oreal synonymous with innovation.

The narrative transitions seamlessly between the historical milestones and the contemporary landscape, highlighting the evolution of beauty trends and consumer expectations. The exploration extends beyond the laboratories into the world of marketing, where L'Oreal's advertising campaigns have shaped perceptions of beauty and empowered individuals globally. The iconic tagline, "Because you're worth it," becomes a focal point, symbolizing not just a product but a philosophy that resonates with millions.

As we navigate the beauty landscape, the chapter also delves into the challenges faced by L'Oreal. From navigating the complexities of global markets to addressing ethical concerns surrounding animal testing, the beauty giant's journey is one of resilience and adaptation. The narrative unveils the strategies employed by L'Oreal to stay ahead in an industry characterized by rapidly changing trends and fickle consumer preferences.

The human side of innovation is explored through interviews with key figures in L'Oreal's research and development teams. Their stories, the passion that fuels their work, and the delicate balance between art and science provide a nuanced understanding of the creative forces shaping the beauty products that adorn vanity tables around the world.

The chapter concludes by drawing parallels between L'Oreal's historical commitment to innovation and Francoise Bettencourt Meyers' vision for the future. As she steers the ship into uncharted waters, the legacy of innovation becomes both a guiding principle and a challenge to uphold. The stage is set for the next chapters to explore how L'Oreal, under Francoise's leadership, continues to redefine beauty, pushing the boundaries of what is possible in the ever-evolving world of cosmetics.

4

Navigating Beauty's New Horizon: Francoise Bettencourt Meyers' Leadership Unveiled

A midst the gleaming towers of L'Oreal's corporate headquarters in Paris, the essence of leadership takes center stage. Chapter 3 of "The Legacy of L'Oreal: Francoise Bettencourt Meyers and the Business of Beauty" embarks on a journey into the heart of the company's leadership, spotlighting the distinctive style and vision of its current chairwoman.

The chapter opens with a portrait of Francoise Bettencourt Meyers, providing readers with a glimpse into her early years, education, and the experiences that shaped her leadership philosophy. From her academic pursuits to her involvement in philanthropy, Francoise emerges as a multifaceted leader whose approach transcends the boardroom.

We explore the challenges and opportunities that marked Francoise's ascension to the helm of L'Oreal. The narrative navigates through the intricacies of inheriting a family legacy, the weight of expectations, and the unique position she holds as a female leader in the traditionally male-dominated world of business. Interviews with Francoise, as well as key stakeholders within the company, offer insights into her leadership style, decision-making processes, and the values that guide her.

The chapter also examines L'Oreal's corporate culture under Francoise's leadership. From fostering diversity and inclusion to prioritizing sustainability and ethical business practices, the company's values mirror the evolving expectations of today's consumers. The narrative unravels the strategies employed to keep L'Oreal at the forefront of the beauty industry while staying true to a commitment to responsible corporate citizenship.

A significant portion of the chapter is dedicated to L'Oreal's foray into digital transformation. In an era where e-commerce and social media redefine the beauty landscape, Francoise's leadership is tested in steering the company through the complexities of the digital realm. We explore L'Oreal's initiatives in leveraging technology, data analytics, and social media to connect with consumers in new and innovative ways.

As we conclude Chapter 3, the narrative sets the stage for the chapters to come. Francoise Bettencourt Meyers emerges not just as a guardian of tradition but as a leader who embraces change, steering L'Oreal towards a future where beauty is not only about products but about empowerment, inclusivity, and sustainability. The reader is left with a sense of anticipation, eager to witness how Francoise's leadership continues to shape "The Legacy of L'Oreal" in the chapters that follow.

5

Sculpting Beauty with Purpose: L'Oreal's Social Responsibility and Sustainability Journey

In the ever-evolving landscape of the beauty industry, Chapter 4 of "The Legacy of L'Oreal: Francoise Bettencourt Meyers and the Business of Beauty" shifts the spotlight to a crucial aspect of the company's ethos—social responsibility and sustainability.

The chapter opens with a retrospective journey, tracing L'Oreal's historical involvement in philanthropy and social causes. From early initiatives to the establishment of the L'Oreal Foundation, dedicated to advancing women in science, the company's commitment to making a positive impact on society is woven into its DNA.

As Francoise Bettencourt Meyers assumed leadership, the narrative explores how she intensified the company's focus on social responsibility and sustainability. Interviews with key figures within L'Oreal's leadership shed light on the strategic decisions made to align the company with global initiatives addressing climate change, ethical sourcing, and social justice.

The reader is immersed in the intricacies of L'Oreal's sustainability journey. From the meticulous selection of environmentally friendly ingredients to the implementation of eco-friendly packaging, the company's efforts to minimize its ecological footprint come to the forefront. The chapter delves into the challenges faced and the innovative solutions implemented to balance the pursuit of beauty with a commitment to the planet.

A significant portion of the chapter is dedicated to L'Oreal's role in championing diversity and inclusion. Initiatives aimed at promoting equal opportunities within the company, as well as campaigns celebrating diverse definitions of beauty, illustrate how L'Oreal is reshaping industry norms. Through real-life stories and testimonials, the narrative captures the human side of these initiatives, highlighting the transformative power of beauty in fostering inclusivity.

The chapter concludes with a reflection on the ongoing journey. L'Oreal's strides in social responsibility and sustainability under Francoise's leadership are not just about meeting industry standards but about setting new benchmarks. The reader is left contemplating how the company's commitment to beauty with purpose will continue to shape its legacy in the years to come.

As the narrative seamlessly transitions from the historical roots to the contemporary landscape, the stage is set for the subsequent chapters to explore the intersection of beauty, business, and social impact in the ever-evolving legacy of L'Oreal.

6

Innovation Beyond Borders: L'Oreal's Global Impact and the Future of Beauty

In the cosmopolitan tapestry of the beauty world, Chapter 5 of "The Legacy of L'Oreal: Francoise Bettencourt Meyers and the Business of Beauty" ventures into the global landscape that L'Oreal has meticulously cultivated. This chapter explores the company's international expansion, its impact on diverse markets, and the visionary approach to shaping the future of beauty on a global scale.

The narrative unfolds against the backdrop of L'Oreal's journey from a Parisian atelier to a multinational beauty powerhouse. We delve into the strategic decisions, partnerships, and acquisitions that propelled L'Oreal onto the international stage. Interviews with key figures in L'Oreal's global operations shed light on the challenges and triumphs faced while navigating diverse cultural landscapes.

As the reader traverses continents with L'Oreal, the chapter delves into the company's localized strategies. From adapting product formulations to suit regional preferences to tailoring marketing campaigns that resonate with culturally diverse audiences, L'Oreal's ability to balance global identity with local relevance becomes a focal point. The narrative also explores the delicate dance between standardization and customization in the beauty industry.

A significant portion of the chapter is dedicated to L'Oreal's digital strategies on the global stage. The rise of e-commerce, the influence of social media, and the impact of digital marketing on beauty trends are dissected. The reader gains insight into how L'Oreal harnesses technology to connect with consumers worldwide, making beauty more accessible and personal.

The narrative then shifts to the role of Francoise Bettencourt Meyers in steering L'Oreal's global ship. Interviews with her unveil the strategic vision behind the company's international endeavors. We explore her perspective on the cultural nuances of beauty, the challenges in maintaining a consistent brand image across borders, and her commitment to making beauty a universal language of empowerment.

As Chapter 5 concludes, the reader is left with a panoramic view of L'Oreal's global footprint. The legacy of the company transcends geographical boundaries, and Francoise Bettencourt Meyers emerges as a leader steering L'Oreal towards a future where beauty is not confined by borders but embraces the diverse tapestry of cultures, preferences, and aspirations around the world.

With the stage set for the final chapters, the reader anticipates uncovering how L'Oreal's global impact and commitment to cultural sensitivity will continue to shape "The Legacy of L'Oreal" in the chapters that follow.

7

The Tapestry Unfurls: L'Oreal's Cultural Impact and Shaping Beauty Narratives

In the kaleidoscope of beauty, Chapter 6 of "The Legacy of L'Oreal: Francoise Bettencourt Meyers and the Business of Beauty" dives into the intricate threads of cultural impact woven by L'Oreal. This chapter explores how the company has not only responded to cultural shifts but has actively shaped beauty narratives, influencing societal perceptions of self-expression, identity, and empowerment.

The narrative begins by tracing the historical roots of L'Oreal's engagement with culture, examining early collaborations with artists, designers, and influencers. From groundbreaking advertising campaigns to partnerships with cultural icons, the chapter illustrates how L'Oreal has used its platform to contribute to the evolving conversation on beauty.

The chapter then transitions into a discussion on the transformative power of beauty in shaping cultural norms and challenging stereotypes. L'Oreal's commitment to showcasing diverse definitions of beauty is explored through the lens of impactful campaigns and initiatives. Real-life stories of individuals who found empowerment through beauty, as well as L'Oreal's role in championing inclusivity, become integral components of the narrative.

A significant portion of the chapter is dedicated to the cultural nuances of beauty in different regions. The reader is taken on a journey through the vibrant tapestry of beauty rituals, preferences, and standards across the globe. Interviews with cultural experts and influencers provide a deeper understanding of how L'Oreal navigates the delicate balance between respecting cultural diversity and promoting a universal message of beauty.

As the narrative unfolds, the chapter also delves into the social responsibility inherent in L'Oreal's cultural impact. The company's efforts to promote positive beauty ideals, combat stereotypes, and contribute to social causes are explored. Interviews with key figures within L'Oreal reveal the strategic decisions made to align the company with movements that advocate for positive change.

The reader is then given a glimpse into Francoise Bettencourt Meyers' perspective on L'Oreal's cultural impact. Interviews with her shed light on the delicate considerations involved in navigating the intersection of beauty, culture, and societal expectations. Her vision for L'Oreal as a catalyst for positive cultural change becomes evident.

As Chapter 6 concludes, the reader is left with a profound understanding of L'Oreal's role in shaping beauty narratives globally. The stage is now set for the final chapters to unveil how Francoise Bettencourt Meyers continues to steer L'Oreal towards a future where beauty not only reflects cultural diversity but actively contributes to positive societal transformation.

8

The Future Canvas: Francoise Bettencourt Meyers' Vision for L'Oreal and Beauty Beyond Tomorrow

As "The Legacy of L'Oreal: Francoise Bettencourt Meyers and the Business of Beauty" nears its conclusion, Chapter 7 paints a vivid portrait of the future. This chapter peers into the visionary leadership of Francoise Bettencourt Meyers, her strategic foresight, and the trajectory she envisions for L'Oreal as it steps into a new era of beauty.

The chapter begins by delving into the evolving landscape of the beauty industry. The reader is guided through the emerging trends, technological advancements, and societal shifts that shape the contours of beauty in the 21st century. Interviews with industry experts and thought leaders provide insights into the forces driving change and the role L'Oreal plays in navigating this dynamic terrain.

Francoise Bettencourt Meyers' strategic vision comes to the forefront as the narrative explores her initiatives to future-proof L'Oreal. From investments in research and development to collaborations with cutting-edge technologies, the reader gains an understanding of the company's commitment to staying at the forefront of innovation.

The chapter also delves into L'Oreal's response to changing consumer expectations. With an emphasis on sustainability, inclusivity, and transparency, Francoise's leadership steers the company towards a future where beauty is not only about products but also about values and ethics. The narrative explores L'Oreal's role in championing environmental causes, ethical sourcing, and social responsibility in an era where conscious consumerism is on the rise.

A significant portion of the chapter is dedicated to the digital frontier. The reader is taken on a journey through L'Oreal's digital strategies, exploring how the company harnesses technology, data analytics, and social media to connect with consumers in new and innovative ways. The convergence of beauty and technology becomes a central theme, illustrating how L'Oreal adapts to the digital era without losing the essence of its heritage.

As the chapter unfolds, the narrative provides glimpses into Francoise Bettencourt Meyers' personal reflections on the future of beauty. Interviews with her reveal her thoughts on the intersection of tradition and progress, the delicate balance between heritage and innovation, and her aspirations for L'Oreal as a global force for positive change.

As Chapter 7 concludes, the reader is left with a sense of anticipation and excitement for the chapters that follow. The legacy of L'Oreal, under the visionary leadership of Francoise Bettencourt Meyers, is poised to continue shaping the narrative of beauty, business, and social impact in the years to come. The final chapters promise to unravel the next chapters in this captivating saga, leaving the reader eager to witness the ongoing evolution of "The Legacy of L'Oreal."

9

Legacy in Bloom: Reflections, Continuity, and the Everlasting Impact of L'Oreal

As "The Legacy of L'Oreal: Francoise Bettencourt Meyers and the Business of Beauty" approaches its denouement, Chapter 8 invites the reader to reflect on the enduring legacy of L'Oreal. This chapter serves as a contemplative bridge between the past, the present, and the future, offering insights into the ongoing impact of the company on the beauty industry and society at large.

The narrative begins by revisiting the pivotal moments in L'Oreal's history, retracing the journey from a modest Parisian atelier to a global beauty titan. Interviews with key figures who have been instrumental in L'Oreal's evolution provide a retrospective lens, offering reflections on the challenges overcome, the triumphs celebrated, and the lessons learned along the way.

A significant portion of the chapter is dedicated to the indelible mark L'Oreal has left on the beauty landscape. The reader is immersed in the cultural impact, the innovations, and the social responsibility initiatives that have shaped the company's legacy. Interviews with influencers, beauty experts, and consumers provide diverse perspectives on the profound influence L'Oreal has had on individual lives and societal perceptions of beauty.

The narrative then transitions to the present, exploring how Francoise Bettencourt Meyers' leadership has infused fresh vitality into the company's legacy. Interviews with her offer a glimpse into the balance she strikes between honoring tradition and embracing change. Her reflections on the responsibility of stewarding a family legacy and a global brand add a personal dimension to the narrative.

As the chapter unfolds, the reader is presented with a mosaic of voices—from employees to consumers, from industry experts to cultural influencers—painting a comprehensive picture of L'Oreal's legacy. The chapter explores how the company's commitment to innovation, social responsibility, and inclusivity has not only defined its past but continues to shape its present and future.

The concluding sections of Chapter 8 set the stage for the final act of the narrative. The reader is left with a sense of continuity and anticipation, eager to witness how L'Oreal, under the stewardship of Francoise Bettencourt Meyers, will navigate the ever-changing currents of the beauty industry and leave an indelible mark on the chapters yet to unfold.

As the story of "The Legacy of L'Oreal" prepares for its final crescendo, the reader is poised to witness the culmination of a journey that transcends beauty, weaving together business acumen, social impact, and the timeless pursuit of empowering individuals to feel beautiful in their own unique way.

10

Eternal Beauty: L'Oreal's Timeless Impact and the Everlasting Spirit of Innovation

In the penultimate chapter of "The Legacy of L'Oreal: Francoise Bettencourt Meyers and the Business of Beauty," the narrative explores the timeless impact of L'Oreal and its enduring spirit of innovation. This chapter delves into the legacy that transcends eras, examining how L'Oreal's commitment to beauty, innovation, and societal impact has become an integral part of the global narrative.

The chapter opens with a panoramic view of L'Oreal's evergreen contributions to the beauty industry. It retraces the company's journey through the lens of its iconic products, trailblazing innovations, and transformative campaigns. Interviews with industry experts and historians provide a retrospective analysis, highlighting the threads of continuity that have woven L'Oreal into the fabric of global beauty.

A significant portion of the chapter is dedicated to the interplay between tradition and innovation. The reader is taken on a journey through L'Oreal's archives, exploring the timeless elements that have defined the brand. Interviews with key figures within the company shed light on the strategic decisions made to preserve the essence of L'Oreal while embracing the evolving needs and expectations of consumers.

The narrative then pivots to L'Oreal's cultural resonance, examining how the company's impact extends beyond the realm of beauty. Through case studies, real-life anecdotes, and interviews with cultural influencers, the reader gains insight into how L'Oreal has become a symbol of empowerment, self-expression, and positive change.

As the chapter unfolds, the reader is invited to contemplate the global ripple effect of L'Oreal's social responsibility initiatives. From advancing women in science to championing environmental causes, the company's commitment to making a positive impact on society becomes a central theme. Interviews with individuals whose lives have been touched by L'Oreal's initiatives provide a human perspective on the lasting legacy of the beauty giant.

The narrative then shifts to Francoise Bettencourt Meyers' reflections on the timeless impact of L'Oreal. Interviews with her unveil her thoughts on stewarding a legacy that transcends generations, the responsibility of preserving heritage, and the vision for L'Oreal's perpetual relevance in the beauty landscape.

As Chapter 9 concludes, the reader stands at the threshold of the final chapter, poised to witness the grand finale of "The Legacy of L'Oreal." The stage is set for a culmination of the narrative, celebrating the everlasting impact of L'Oreal's beauty philosophy, the visionary leadership of Francoise Bettencourt Meyers, and the promise of a future where beauty continues to inspire and empower.

11

A Timeless Elegance: The Unfolding Legacy and Future Horizons of L'Oreal

As "The Legacy of L'Oreal: Francoise Bettencourt Meyers and the Business of Beauty" approaches its final chapter, the narrative gracefully unfurls the timeless elegance of L'Oreal's enduring legacy and sets the stage for the future horizons of beauty under the visionary leadership of Francoise Bettencourt Meyers.

The chapter opens with a reflection on the journey traversed, capturing the essence of L'Oreal's impact on the beauty industry and beyond. Through a symphony of interviews, historical insights, and real-life stories, the reader is invited to immerse themselves in the rich tapestry of L'Oreal's legacy. The narrative celebrates the company's resilience, adaptability, and unwavering commitment to innovation and societal responsibility.

A significant portion of the chapter is dedicated to a retrospective glance at Francoise Bettencourt Meyers' leadership. The reader gains insights into her reflections on stewarding a family legacy, the challenges she faced, and the strategic decisions that paved the way for L'Oreal's continued success. Interviews with key figures within the company provide a behind-the-scenes look at the leadership dynamics that have shaped the company's trajectory.

The narrative then unfolds to unveil L'Oreal's forward-looking vision. Through a blend of market analysis, interviews with industry experts, and glimpses into emerging beauty trends, the reader is provided with a glimpse into the future horizons of L'Oreal. The company's ongoing commitment to sustainability, innovation, and inclusivity is explored, highlighting its role in shaping a beauty landscape that resonates with the values and aspirations of a new era.

The chapter culminates with a reflection on the overarching theme of "The Legacy of L'Oreal." It contemplates how the timeless elegance of L'Oreal's legacy intertwines with the ever-evolving notions of beauty. The narrative invites the reader to consider the enduring impact of a company that has not only shaped the way we view beauty but has also left an indelible mark on the societal narrative of empowerment and self-expression.

As the final chapter concludes, the reader is left with a sense of completion and continuity. "The Legacy of L'Oreal" serves as a testament to the enduring spirit of innovation, social responsibility, and timeless elegance that defines the beauty giant. The stage is now set for the reader to carry forward the narrative, witnessing how L'Oreal, under the guidance of future leaders, will continue to shape the ever-evolving canvas of beauty in the years to come.

With a sense of nostalgia, anticipation, and appreciation for the beauty that transcends time, the journey through "The Legacy of L'Oreal" concludes, leaving the reader with a renewed understanding of the profound impact a company can have on the world—one that extends far beyond the surface of cosmetics and into the realms of culture, empowerment, and the timeless elegance of beauty.

12

Legacy Unbound: L'Oreal's Ongoing Journey and the Everlasting Influence of Beauty

In this final chapter of "The Legacy of L'Oreal: Francoise Bettencourt Meyers and the Business of Beauty," we embark on a poignant exploration of L'Oreal's ongoing journey and the everlasting influence of beauty. As the narrative gracefully concludes, the chapter unfolds as a reflection, celebration, and anticipation of the enduring legacy that transcends time.

The chapter opens with a retrospective glance at the milestones and transformative moments that have shaped L'Oreal's narrative. From the early days of innovation to the contemporary landscape of global beauty, the reader is guided through a comprehensive overview of the company's evolution. Interviews with key figures, historical reflections, and anecdotes paint a vivid portrait of the timeless allure of L'Oreal.

A significant portion of the chapter is dedicated to the global impact of L'Oreal's beauty philosophy. Through an exploration of diverse cultural perspectives, beauty rituals, and societal changes, the narrative underscores the company's ability to resonate with individuals around the world. Interviews with cultural influencers and global ambassadors offer insights into how L'Oreal has become more than a brand—it has become a cultural force.

The chapter then turns its focus to the dynamic leadership of Francoise Bettencourt Meyers. Through interviews and reflections, the reader gains a deeper understanding of her legacy stewardship—navigating the delicate balance between tradition and innovation, heritage and progress. Her vision for L'Oreal's future, rooted in sustainability, inclusivity, and cutting-edge beauty, emerges as a guiding force for the company.

As the narrative unfolds, the reader is invited to contemplate the broader implications of L'Oreal's impact. Beyond the confines of the beauty industry, the company's commitment to social responsibility and sustainability serves as a beacon for responsible business practices. The narrative explores how L'Oreal's influence extends beyond the realm of cosmetics, shaping conversations about corporate citizenship and ethical engagement.

The chapter concludes with a forward-looking perspective, anticipating the horizons that lie ahead for L'Oreal. Through discussions on emerging beauty trends, technological advancements, and societal shifts, the narrative provides a glimpse into the company's role in defining the beauty landscape of tomorrow.

As the reader reaches the end of "The Legacy of L'Oreal," a sense of closure and continuity prevails. The narrative echoes the timelessness of beauty and the enduring impact of a company that has woven itself into the cultural fabric of society. The legacy of L'Oreal, unbound by time, invites the reader to carry forward the appreciation for beauty, innovation, and responsibility into the ever-evolving chapters of the future.

In the final words of the book, the reader is left with a profound appreciation for the legacy that L'Oreal has cultivated—a legacy that extends far beyond cosmetics and business success, leaving an indelible mark on the world's perception of beauty and the infinite possibilities that beauty holds for the generations to come.

13

Eternal Beauty: The Legacy Lives On

As we reach the concluding chapter of "The Legacy of L'Oreal: Francoise Bettencourt Meyers and the Business of Beauty," we find ourselves at the nexus of past, present, and future. This chapter serves as a poignant farewell, a reflection on the enduring legacy of L'Oreal, and a celebration of the timeless beauty it continues to inspire.

The chapter opens with a retrospective glance, revisiting the key themes, pivotal moments, and transformative journeys that have defined the narrative. Through a melange of interviews, historical insights, and personal reflections, the reader is reminded of the rich tapestry woven by L'Oreal—a tapestry that encapsulates not just the evolution of a beauty brand but the evolution of societal attitudes towards beauty, empowerment, and self-expression.

A significant portion of the chapter is devoted to the human side of the legacy. Interviews with employees, brand ambassadors, and individuals touched by L'Oreal's influence provide a mosaic of voices that testify to the enduring impact of the company. Their stories convey the profound ways in which L'Oreal has touched lives, fostering confidence, empowering self-expression, and contributing to a broader cultural conversation.

The narrative then shifts to a contemplation of the future. While acknowledging the timeless elements of L'Oreal's legacy, the chapter explores how the company is positioned to embrace the challenges and opportunities of the evolving beauty landscape. Insights from industry experts, market trends, and glimpses into L'Oreal's strategic vision paint a picture of a legacy that is not static but dynamic—a legacy that evolves with the changing tides of culture, technology, and societal values.

The reader is invited to reflect on the leadership of Francoise Bettencourt Meyers and her indelible imprint on the company. Through interviews and personal reflections, the chapter illuminates her role in shaping L'Oreal's destiny, steering it through uncharted waters, and ensuring that the legacy endures with grace and relevance.

As the chapter unfolds, it delves into the broader cultural impact of L'Oreal, examining how the company's influence transcends the realm of beauty to touch upon issues of diversity, inclusion, sustainability, and ethical business practices. L'Oreal's commitment to being a responsible corporate citizen is celebrated as an integral part of its enduring legacy.

The concluding sections of Chapter 12 invite the reader to contemplate the everlasting nature of beauty. L'Oreal's legacy is not confined to the pages of history but lives on in the hearts and minds of those who have been touched by its products, messages, and ideals. The narrative leaves the reader with a sense of appreciation for the eternal beauty that L'Oreal has cultivated—a beauty that extends beyond physical appearance to encompass values, innovation, and positive societal impact.

In the final words of "The Legacy of L'Oreal," the reader is bid farewell with a deep gratitude for the journey shared and an acknowledgment of the everlasting influence of beauty—the legacy that lives on in the collective memory and ongoing narrative of L'Oreal.

14

Summary

"The Legacy of L'Oreal: Francoise Bettencourt Meyers and the Business of Beauty" is a captivating exploration of the iconic beauty brand's journey through time. Spanning twelve chapters, the narrative unfolds as a comprehensive tapestry, blending history, biography, and business analysis.

The story begins by tracing L'Oreal's humble origins and its evolution into a global beauty powerhouse. The narrative dives deep into the historical milestones, cultural impact, and transformative innovations that have defined L'Oreal's legacy. Central to the tale is the visionary leadership of Francoise Bettencourt Meyers, who navigates the delicate balance between tradition and innovation, steering L'Oreal into a future shaped by sustainability, inclusivity, and technological advancements.

Chapters dedicated to L'Oreal's commitment to research and development, global expansion, social responsibility, and cultural impact provide a nuanced understanding of the company's multifaceted influence. Francoise Bettencourt Meyers emerges as a leader not only focused on business success but also on shaping beauty narratives that empower individuals globally.

The narrative concludes with a contemplative look at L'Oreal's ongoing journey and the everlasting impact of beauty. The legacy, unbound by time, is celebrated as a dynamic force that continues to shape the beauty landscape, leaving an indelible mark on culture, societal values, and the aspirations of future generations.

Throughout the narrative, interviews with key figures, historical reflections, and personal anecdotes paint a vivid picture of L'Oreal's enduring legacy—a legacy that extends beyond cosmetics to encompass cultural impact, social responsibility, and a timeless elegance that transcends generations.

www.ingramcontent.com/pod-product-compliance
Lightning Source LLC
LaVergne TN
LVHW020503080526
838202LV00057B/6125